INVEST AI
QUANTUM

Top Quantum Computing, Machine Learning, Autonomous, Cloud Computing, and AI Companies Shaping the Future of Investing

POP BUCHANAN

Cover Design by German Creative.

Book Design and Production by Josephe Raymond Buchanan

Consultant: Jennifer Ruff

Photos: Meta is Dope

ISBN: 978-1-7346798-5-4

Table of Contents

1

Disclaimer

The information in this book is speculative and hypothetical and intended for entertainment and educational purposes only. It is not intended to be, nor should it be construed as, fact, financial advice, investment recommendations, or guidance. Any investment decisions made based on the content of this book are done so at your own risk.

We do not guarantee specific investment outcomes, financial returns, or success in the financial markets. Any strategies discussed in this book are purely educational and should not be considered a recommendation for any specific investment action.

Readers are strongly encouraged to conduct due diligence, research, and analysis before making investment decisions. Consulting with a qualified financial advisor, fiduciary, or professional to assess individual investment objectives, risk tolerance, and financial situation is recommended.

The author, POP Buchanan, and Invest AI are not liable for any investment losses, financial damages, or adverse outcomes resulting from using the information in this book. Additionally, any references to AI or the use of AI in the editorial aspects of writing

2
What is Quantum Computing?

Quantum computing is a groundbreaking technology that capitalizes on the principles of quantum mechanics, enabling computations and simulations at an exponentially accelerated pace and efficiency compared to traditional computers. By utilizing quantum bits (qubits), quantum computers can tackle intricate problems once deemed unsolvable or demanded an impractical timeframe for classical computers. This transformative potential extends across numerous domains, including cryptography, drug discovery, climate modeling, and artificial intelligence, heralding a new era of scientific progress and innovation.

3
Why Invest In Quantum

Expanding upon the insights garnered from our inaugural book, "Invest AI: The Last Gold Rush in AI Stock Investments," we embark on the next leg of our journey with "Invest AI: Quantum." Suited for both seasoned investors and novices alike, this sequel is tailored for those already acquainted with AI and investment landscapes, now eager to explore the potential of Quantum Computing. Geared towards all readers, including the "Quantum Curious," this book aims to furnish them with the requisite tools and insights to navigate the intricate realm of quantum technologies. As in our first publication, we'll unearth promising opportunities for innovation and disruption, this time at the intersection of Quantum Computing and AI. Join us as we unravel this technical landscape and translate knowledge into actionable investment ideas. Welcome to "Invest AI: Quantum."

4

Michio Kaku and the Power of Quantum Computing

Disclaimer: Michio Kaku does not endorse investing in quantum computing, and any mention of his thoughts or quotes in this book is for educational purposes only.

The profound insights American Astrophysicist and Science Writer Michio Kaku shared regarding the potential of quantum computing have been a primary inspiration for creating the Invest AI: Quantum Computer book. Kaku's elucidation of concepts such as quantum supremacy and exponential speedup has underscored the transformative power of quantum computing in reshaping computation and problem-solving paradigms. "By 2100, our destiny is to become like the gods we once worshipped and feared. But our tools will not be magic wands and potions but the science of computers, nanotechnology, artificial intelligence, biotechnology, and most of all, the quantum theory."

— **Michio Kaku,** Physics of the Future: How Science Will Shape Human Destiny and Our Daily Lives by the Year 2100, Kaku asserts his visionary perspective on the future. Understanding the societal impact outlined by Kaku, including advancements in scientific research and potential disruptions in cybersecurity, has prompted a fun examination of quantum computing's potential role in financial markets and investment opportunities. The book aims to provide investors with a basic understanding of quantum computing technology and its implications, empowering them to navigate the evolving landscape of AI-driven investment strategies.

5
Welcome to the Power of Quantum

We are on the cusp of a technological tsunami transforming our world in ways we never thought possible. Quantum Computing (QP) and Artificial Intelligence (AI) are the twin engines driving this revolution and are poised to change everything.

QP is harnessing the power of atoms and subatomic particles to perform calculations that were previously unimaginable. AI enables machines to learn, reason, and adapt in ways previously the exclusive domain of humans.

Together, QP and AI are creating a new era of innovation where complex problems are being solved, new industries are emerging, and how we live, work, and play is redefined.

This book will take you on a summarized journey through the groundbreaking world of QP and AI. We will explore the fundamentals of these technologies, their applications, and the exciting developments shaping our future.

This book is for tech enthusiasts, avid investors, or anyone curious about the future.

6

Quantum Computing Trends

As of today, several noteworthy developments have shaped the landscape in quantum computing.

Firstly, there's a growing concern about the need for quantum-based encryption solutions to address potential security risks. The fear of malicious actors exploiting quantum computing to decrypt data in the future has led to the exploration of quantum-resistant security alternatives for data transmission.

Secondly, the rise of Quantum Computing as a Service (QCaaS) is gaining momentum. Cloud computing platforms like IBM, Microsoft Azure, Google Cloud, and AWS Braket are democratizing access to quantum computational power. Companies also consider private cloud and hosted services to meet stringent data privacy requirements.

Thirdly, governments worldwide are committing substantial funding to advance quantum research, exceeding $40 billion over the next decade. This investment aims to establish several new national quantum research centers, fostering innovation and development in quantum technology.

Additionally, the discussion around physical and logical qubits is gaining attention. Simone Severini, General Manager of Quantum Technologies at AWS and UCL, emphasizes the importance of logical qubits' performance and clock speed in quantum computing. Advancements in this area are leading toward the Logical Intermediate-Scale Quantum (LISQ) era, focusing on optimizing fidelity, clock speed, and error correction.

Lastly, the concept of a quantum internet, leveraging quantum mechanics for communication, is emerging as WEB 2.0. While widespread implementation may take time, discussions around it have intensified, especially with China's notable progress in this field.

7

Quantum for Enthusiasts and Entrepreneurs: Seizing Opportunities in QP

Accessing quantum computing, investing in the field, or starting a small business related to quantum computing can be challenging but feasible with the right approach. Here's a general roadmap for individuals interested in capitalizing on quantum computing:

- Education and Training: Start by gaining a solid understanding of quantum computing principles, algorithms, and applications. Various online courses, tutorials, and educational resources are available, including platforms like Coursera, edX, and Quantum Open Source Foundation (QOSF). Consider enrolling in formal education programs specializing in quantum computing offered by universities or research institutions.

- Networking and Community Engagement: Join quantum computing communities, forums, and social media groups to connect with experts, researchers, and enthusiasts. Participate in workshops, conferences, and meetups to stay updated on the latest developments and opportunities in quantum computing. Networking can also lead to potential collaborations or mentorship opportunities.

- Access to Quantum Computing Resources: While building your expertise, explore platforms that offer access to quantum computing resources for experimentation and learning. Companies like IBM (IBM Quantum Experience), Google (Cirq), Microsoft (Azure Quantum), and Amazon (Braket) provide cloud-based quantum computing services and development tools accessible to individuals and businesses.

- Research and Innovation: Identify specific areas within quantum computing where you can contribute or innovate. This could involve developing new algorithms, software applications, or hardware components tailored to address industry needs or research challenges. Collaborate with universities, research institutions, or industry partners to explore novel solutions and potential commercialization opportunities.

- Investment and Entrepreneurship: Consider investing in quantum computing startups, venture capital funds, or publicly traded companies active in the quantum computing space. Conduct thorough research to understand the market landscape, technology trends, and investment opportunities. Alternatively, if you have a viable business idea or innovation, explore options for starting a quantum computing-related venture. This could involve securing funding, building a team, and developing a business plan to bring your idea to market.

- Stay Informed and Adapt: Quantum computing is a rapidly evolving field, so it's essential to stay informed about advancements, regulatory changes, and market dynamics. Continuously update your skills, knowledge, and strategies to adapt to emerging trends and seize opportunities as they arise.

Building expertise in quantum computing and navigating the associated opportunities may require time, dedication, and persistence. However, with passion, commitment, and strategic planning, individuals can capitalize on quantum computing's transformative potential and contribute to shaping its future impact across industries.

8
Quantum Computing and Artificial Intelligence

The convergence of **Quantum Computing (QP)** and **Artificial Intelligence (AI)** represents a pivotal moment in technological advancement, offering unprecedented opportunities for innovation and problem-solving across various domains. By harnessing the unparalleled processing capabilities of quantum computers and the adaptive intelligence of AI systems, we can confront complex challenges that were once deemed insurmountable. Think "ATLANTIS".

- **Optimization**: Quantum computing's inherent parallelism and ability to explore multiple solutions simultaneously make it ideally suited for optimization problems. AI algorithms can leverage this capability to optimize processes, resource allocation, and logistics in finance and manufacturing industries, increasing efficiency and cost savings.

- **Machine Learning**: Quantum computing can accelerate the training and execution of machine learning models by processing vast datasets and complex algorithms more efficiently. This synergy enables AI systems to extract deeper insights, make more accurate predictions, and uncover patterns in data that were previously elusive, driving advancements in fields like healthcare, finance, and autonomous systems.

- **Natural Language Processing (NLP):** Quantum-enhanced algorithms can enhance the speed and accuracy of natural language processing tasks, enabling AI systems to understand, interpret, and generate human language with greater precision. This has profound implications for applications such as virtual assistants, language translation, and sentiment analysis, facilitating more seamless human-machine interactions.

- **Computer Vision:** Quantum computing can revolutionize computer vision by enabling the rapid analysis of complex visual data, such as images and videos, with unprecedented speed and accuracy. AI-powered vision systems can leverage quantum algorithms to detect real-time patterns, objects, and anomalies, leading to advancements in surveillance, healthcare imaging, and autonomous driving.

While the fusion of QP and AI holds immense promise, it poses significant challenges and ethical considerations. Concerns about data privacy, algorithmic bias, and the responsible use of AI-powered technologies must be addressed to ensure equitable and transparent outcomes. As we navigate this dynamic landscape, it is essential to approach the integration of quantum computing and artificial intelligence with careful consideration of both the opportunities and risks involved.

9

Origins of Quantum Computing

Quantum computing, born from the minds of academia and industry, represents a collaborative endeavor poised to redefine the boundaries of computation. Pioneers such as John Preskill, Dario Gil, Freeke Heijman, and IBM have pivotal roles in nurturing this revolutionary technology. Emerging from the esoteric realm of quantum mechanics, quantum computing promises to unlock unprecedented computational power with transformative implications across diverse fields such as chemistry, materials science, and artificial intelligence.

The genesis of quantum computing can be traced back to the foundational principles of quantum mechanics, where the counterintuitive behavior of particles at the quantum level laid the groundwork for a paradigm shift in computing. Unlike classical computers that operate on binary bits, quantum computers harness the peculiar properties of quantum bits or qubits, such as superposition and entanglement, to perform computations in ways previously deemed impossible.

With the potential to solve complex problems exponentially faster than classical computers, quantum computing stands to revolutionize industries such as drug discovery, where the simulation of molecular interactions could lead to the development of life-saving medications. Similarly, in climate modeling, quantum algorithms could enable more accurate predictions of climate patterns, facilitating proactive measures to mitigate the impacts of climate change.

However, alongside its boundless potential, the advent of quantum computing also raises profound societal and ethical considerations. The implications of quantum computing on data security, cryptography, and privacy must be carefully evaluated to safeguard against potential risks and vulnerabilities in an increasingly interconnected world.

In this innovation landscape, IBM emerges as a trailblazer in quantum computing, spearheading advancements with groundbreaking achievements such as the 433-qubit Osprey chip and a visionary roadmap for future development. With a commitment to pushing the boundaries of quantum computing and unlocking new frontiers of exploration, IBM's contributions inspire the continued evolution of this transformative technology. As quantum computing continues to mature, its impact on society and the world will be profound, shaping the future of computation and unlocking new realms of possibility.

10

Invest IBM: A Leader in Quantum Computing

IBM is an unparalleled leader in quantum computing, spearheading innovation and propelling the field forward with steadfast dedication. Since its inception in the 1980s, IBM has consistently been at the forefront of quantum computing, shaping its trajectory through groundbreaking contributions across various fronts:

- Quantum Processor Development: IBM's relentless pursuit of quantum processor development has yielded remarkable progress, culminating in cutting-edge quantum chips boasting impressive qubit counts.
- Quantum Algorithms and Software: Through rigorous research and development efforts, IBM has devised sophisticated quantum algorithms and software frameworks, unlocking new avenues for computational exploration and problem-solving.
- Quantum Computing Services and Platforms: IBM's commitment extends beyond mere technological advancement; the company has pioneered quantum computing services and platforms, democratizing access to quantum resources and fostering collaboration across diverse domains.

- Collaborations and Partnerships: Recognizing the collaborative nature of quantum research, IBM has actively engaged in partnerships with academic institutions, research organizations, and industry leaders, amplifying the collective efforts to unravel the mysteries of quantum computing.

IBM's unwavering dedication to quantum computing has borne fruit in the form of groundbreaking achievements, exemplified by the development of cutting-edge quantum processors like the 53-qubit Quantum Falcon and the groundbreaking 433-qubit Osprey chip. Moreover, IBM's quantum computing platform, IBM Quantum, stands as a beacon of accessibility and innovation, offering researchers, developers, and businesses unprecedented access to quantum resources, simulations, and tools.

As we delve into quantum investment, IBM emerges as a cornerstone, driving the frontiers of scientific discovery and technological advancement. With a rich legacy of innovation and an unwavering commitment to excellence, IBM sets the stage for a new era of quantum-powered possibilities.

11

IBM Quantum: Unlocking Quantum Computing's Potential

IBM Quantum is a key platform offering unparalleled access to quantum computers, simulations, and tools that reshape the technological landscape. Critical aspects of IBM Quantum include:

- Quantum Computing Services: Providing cloud-based access to quantum processors and simulators, enabling users to explore the realms of quantum computation.

- Quantum Algorithms and Software: Facilitating the development and execution of quantum algorithms, empowering researchers and developers to harness the power of quantum computing.

- Quantum-Classical Hybrids: They are pioneering the integration of classical and quantum computing techniques, leading to groundbreaking breakthroughs in various fields.

- Quantum Computing Applications: Addressing intricate challenges across industries such as finance, healthcare, and materials science, laying the foundation for transformative solutions.

Investing in IBM Quantum presents a strategic opportunity to capitalize on the burgeoning quantum computing landscape:

- Join the IBM Quantum Network: Collaborate with IBM and industry leaders to drive innovation and advance quantum technologies.
- Develop Quantum Skills: Engage in online courses and workshops to cultivate expertise in quantum computing, positioning yourself at the forefront of this revolutionary field.
- Leverage Quantum-Based Solutions: Utilize IBM Quantum's resources and expertise to develop and deploy quantum-powered solutions, driving impactful outcomes in diverse domains.
- Support Quantum Startups: Invest in innovative companies leveraging IBM Quantum, fostering growth and catalyzing advancements in quantum technology.

By embracing IBM Quantum and its ecosystem, investors can align themselves with the forefront of the quantum computing revolution, poised to shape industries and society with transformative innovations.

12

QP Hardware Companies

Top Companies Manufacturing Quantum Computing Hardware, including both public and private companies, along with their stock symbols (if applicable):

1. IBM (NYSE: IBM)
2. D-Wave Systems (QBTS)
3. Google (Alphabet Inc.) (NASDAQ: GOOGL)
4. Microsoft (NASDAQ: MSFT)
5. Intel (NASDAQ: INTC)
6. ColdQuanta
7. Bleximo
8. Archer Materials (ASX: AXE)
9. Aurora Quantum Technologies
10. AegiQ
11. Alice&Bob
12. Alpine Quantum Technologies
13. Bluefors
14. BraneCell Systems
15. Delft Circuits

These companies are at the forefront of developing various quantum computing hardware components, including quantum processors, qubits, control electronics, and quantum memory devices. Moreover, some entities focus on specific quantum computing applications, such as quantum simulators or solutions for quantum-resistant cryptography.

13

QP Software Companies

Quantum Computing Software companies with their corresponding stock symbols:

1. IBM (NYSE: IBM)
2. Google (Alphabet Inc.) (NASDAQ: GOOGL)
3. Microsoft (NASDAQ: MSFT)
4. Rigetti Computing
5. Xanadu
6. Zapata Computing
7. Q-CTRL
8. QC Ware Corp.
9. Riverlane
10. Quantum Benchmark Inc.
11. Cambridge Quantum Computing
12. Strangeworks
13. Entropica Labs
14. Aliro Quantum
15. 1Qbit

Please note that not all companies listed are publicly traded, so stock symbols may not apply to all.

Cloud Computing, Quantum Computing, and AI: Interconnected Technologies Shaping the Future

Cloud computing revolutionizes the delivery of computing services by providing on-demand access to computing resources over the Internet, including infrastructure, platforms, and software. This model intersects with quantum computing and AI, creating opportunities for innovation.

- Quantum Computing in the Cloud: Leading cloud providers such as IBM, Google, and Microsoft offer quantum computing services, allowing users to remotely access quantum computers and simulations. This democratizes access to quantum computing resources, fostering experimentation and innovation in quantum algorithms and applications.

- AI and Machine Learning in the Cloud: Cloud computing platforms facilitate the deployment and scalability of AI and machine learning models. These models can analyze vast datasets generated by quantum computing experiments, helping researchers extract valuable insights and optimize quantum computing algorithms for real-world applications.

- Quantum AI: The convergence of quantum computing and AI opens new frontiers in solving complex problems. Quantum algorithms, powered by AI techniques such as machine learning, hold promise for accelerating drug discovery, climate modeling, optimization, and other computationally intensive tasks.

- Hybrid Quantum-Classical Computing: Cloud computing enables the integration of classical and quantum computing resources, leading to the development of hybrid quantum-classical algorithms. This approach harnesses the strengths of both computing paradigms to tackle challenges beyond the capabilities of classical or quantum computers alone.

Cloud computing is a foundational infrastructure for advancing quantum computing, AI research, and applications in this dynamic landscape. By providing flexible and scalable resources, cloud providers empower researchers, developers, and businesses to explore the frontiers of these transformative technologies.

Top AI Cloud Computing Companies with Stock Symbols:

1. Amazon (AMZN)
2. Microsoft (MSFT)
3. Google (GOOGL)
4. IBM (IBM)
5. Salesforce (CRM)

14

Practical Applications of Quantum Computing and AI

This chapter explores hypothetical and real-world applications of quantum computing and artificial intelligence (AI), showcasing their potential to revolutionize industries and address real-world challenges.

Here's a breakdown of key areas:

• Quantum Machine Learning: Hypothetical scenarios illustrate how quantum algorithms like quantum k-means and support vector machines could transform tasks in computer vision and natural language processing. For instance, while Car and EV manufacturers are exploring quantum algorithms for traffic flow optimization, actual implementation may still be in the research stage.

• Quantum-Inspired AI: We examine the symbiotic relationship between classical machine learning and quantum computing, where classical techniques enhance quantum algorithms and vice versa. A real-world example includes Google's utilization of quantum-like neural networks to enhance speech recognition accuracy in its products.

• AI-Driven Quantum Computing: Explore how machine learning techniques shape quantum computing, optimizing processes such as tuning quantum gates and simulating quantum systems. Another hypothetical example is in the pharmaceutical industry, where companies like Biogen (illustrative purposes only) are exploring the potential of AI-driven quantum computing to expedite drug discovery through more accurate modeling of molecular interactions.

• Real-World Quantum AI Applications showcase practical implementations of quantum AI across various industries. For instance, while JP Morgan Chase is a leader in AI-driven portfolio optimization, specific details regarding utilizing quantum AI algorithms may be speculative.

15
Quantum Machine Learning

The landscape of quantum machine learning involves the integration of quantum computing principles with traditional machine learning techniques, leading to the development of new algorithms and models. Key players in this field include *Google, Amazon, Microsoft, IBM, Facebook, NVIDIA, OpenAI, Apple, DeepMind (Acquired by Google), and Salesforce*, which are pioneering innovative AI solutions across industries.

Recent advancements have introduced significant algorithms in quantum machine learning:

- Quantum K-Means: An adaptation of the k-means clustering algorithm optimized for handling large datasets efficiently using quantum principles.

- Quantum Support Vector Machines: Quantum-based support vector machines excel in classification and regression tasks, offering improved accuracy and efficiency compared to classical methods.

- Quantum Neural Networks: Leveraging quantum principles, these networks tackle tasks like image recognition and natural language processing with promising capabilities in learning from data.

16

Applications of quantum machine learning span various domains:

- Computer Vision: Enhancing tasks such as image recognition, object detection, and image processing with advanced algorithms.
- Natural Language Processing: Improving language modeling, sentiment analysis, and text classification with higher accuracy and efficiency.
- Materials Science: Accelerating material and drug discovery by simulating complex quantum systems, facilitating novel solutions in scientific research.

Despite promising opportunities, quantum machine learning faces challenges:

- Quantum Noise: Errors inherent in quantum computing can affect algorithm accuracy, requiring robust error correction methods.
- Scalability: Current limitations in quantum computers' qubit count and computational power hinder the effective scaling of quantum machine learning algorithms.

- Quantum-Classical Interfaces: Seamless integration of quantum and classical systems is crucial for practical applications, necessitating innovative approaches to interface design.

Despite challenges, quantum machine learning offers fertile ground for exploration and innovation. As quantum computing technology advances, groundbreaking advancements and practical implementations in quantum machine learning are anticipated. Investors interested in this transformative field should monitor leading companies like *IBM, Google, Amazon, and Microsoft*, driving the evolution of quantum machine learning.

17

Investing in Quantum Computing Companies: A Future-Proof Strategy

Disclaimer: The reader acknowledges and agrees that POP Buchanan and Invest AI are not responsible for any consequences arising from interpreting or applying the information provided in this book.

In today's rapidly evolving technological landscape, investing in quantum computing (QP) companies offers a forward-thinking approach to portfolio diversification and future-proofing investment decisions. As we've explored throughout this book, the convergence of quantum computing and artificial intelligence (AI) presents unprecedented opportunities for innovation and disruption across various industries. Let's translate this technical insight into actionable investment strategies for the Invest AI audience.

Why Invest in Quantum Computing Companies?

- Pioneering Technological Advancements: Quantum computing companies are at the forefront of technological innovation, driving groundbreaking advancements in computation, cryptography, and data analysis. By investing in these companies, investors gain exposure to cutting-edge technologies poised to reshape industries and revolutionize how we live and work.

- Potential for Exponential Growth: Quantum computing holds the potential for exponential growth, with forecasts suggesting that the market could reach billions of dollars in the coming years. Investing in QP companies early allows investors to capitalize on this growth potential and realize significant returns on investment as the technology matures and gains mainstream adoption.

- Diversification Benefits: Including QP companies in an investment portfolio provides diversification benefits, mitigating risks associated with traditional asset classes. As quantum computing continues to gain prominence, diversified portfolios that include exposure to QP companies may offer enhanced risk-adjusted returns over the long term.

Gaining Exposure to Quantum Computing Companies

- Direct Investment: Investors can directly invest in publicly traded QP companies listed on stock exchanges. Conduct thorough research to identify promising companies with strong leadership, innovative technologies, and a competitive edge in the QP market.

- Indirect Investment: Alternatively, investors can gain exposure to QP companies through exchange-traded funds (ETFs) or mutual funds focused on technology or innovation. These investment vehicles offer diversified exposure to a basket of QP companies, reducing individual stock-specific risks.

- Venture Capital and Private Equity: For investors seeking early-stage opportunities, venture capital and private equity funds specializing in quantum computing startups provide access to promising companies at their inception. While these investments entail higher risks, they also offer the potential for substantial returns if successful.

Investing in quantum computing companies represents a strategic allocation of capital towards transformative technologies with the potential to shape the future. By gaining exposure to QP companies, investors position themselves at the forefront of innovation, diversify their portfolios, and capitalize on the exponential growth prospects of quantum computing. As we navigate the intersection of quantum computing and AI, savvy investors recognize the value of incorporating QP companies into their investment strategies, paving the way for future-proof investment decisions and long-term wealth creation.

18

Top 20 publicly traded Quantum Computing AI companies with their stock symbols

Disclaimer: The reader acknowledges and agrees that POP Buchanan and Invest AI are not responsible for any consequences arising from interpreting or applying the information provided in this book.

Welcome to the forefront of the Quantum technology! In this era of unprecedented innovation, quantum computing stands as the pinnacle of human ingenuity, promising to reshape industries, redefine possibilities, and unlock the secrets of the universe. As we embark on this tech journey, join us in exploring the top 20 publicly traded Quantum Computing AI companies. From IonQ's cutting-edge trapped-ion technology to IBM's pioneering research initiatives, these companies drive the quantum revolution forward, propelling us into a future limited only by imagination.

1. IonQ (IONQ): IonQ specializes in trapped-ion quantum computing, aiming to develop scalable quantum computers with high-fidelity qubits.

2. **IBM (IBM):** IBM is a key player in quantum computing, focusing on advancing quantum hardware, software, and algorithms through its IBM Quantum program.

3. **FormFactor (FORM):** FormFactor provides semiconductor test and measurement solutions, including product-characterizing quantum computing devices.

4. **Microsoft (MSFT):** Microsoft is heavily invested in quantum computing research and is developing software tools and cloud services to support quantum computing applications.

5. **Intel (INTC):** Intel is exploring various approaches to quantum computing, including superconducting qubits and silicon spin qubits, as part of its broader research efforts.

6. **Honeywell (HON):** Honeywell is developing trapped-ion quantum computing technology focusing on scalability and commercialization.

7. **Defiance Quantum ETF (QTUM):** The Defiance Quantum ETF is an exchange-traded fund that invests in companies involved in quantum computing and related technologies.

8. **Rigetti Computing (RGTI):** Rigetti Computing is developing quantum processors and quantum cloud services to build practical quantum computers for diverse applications.

9. **Arqit Quantum (ARQQ):** Arqit Quantum focuses on quantum encryption and secure communications, leveraging quantum technology to enhance cybersecurity.

10. Quantum Computing Inc. (QUBT): Quantum Computing Inc. provides quantum-ready applications and solutions, facilitating the integration of quantum computing into existing workflows.

11. Nvidia Corporation (NVDA): Nvidia is known for its GPUs, which are increasingly used for quantum computing simulations and AI applications.

12. D-Wave Systems Inc. (DWV): D-Wave Systems focuses on developing quantum annealing technology for optimization problems and machine learning.

13. Alphabet Inc. (GOOGL): Alphabet, Google's parent company, has invested in quantum computing research through its Quantum AI Lab and research initiatives.

14. Hewlett Packard Enterprise Company (HPE): HPE is exploring quantum computing concepts, such as developing novel qubit technologies and quantum computing platforms.

15. Lockheed Martin Corporation (LMT): Lockheed Martin is involved in quantum computing research for defense and aerospace applications, exploring quantum computing's potential for optimization and simulation tasks.

16. Northrop Grumman Corporation (NOC): Northrop Grumman is researching quantum computing applications for defense and national security, focusing on encryption, communications, and cybersecurity.

17. Raytheon Technologies Corporation (RTX): Raytheon Technologies is exploring quantum computing's potential for defense and aerospace applications, including optimization, simulation, and secure communications.

18. Cisco Systems, Inc. (CSCO): Cisco invests in quantum computing research to explore potential networking, security, and data processing applications.

19. Alibaba Group Holding Limited (BABA): Alibaba is exploring quantum computing research and applications through its Alibaba Quantum Laboratory, focusing on cryptography, optimization, and cloud computing.

20. Tencent Holdings Limited (TCEHY): Tencent is investing in quantum computing research and development, exploring potential applications in cryptography, AI, and cloud computing.

These companies play various roles in advancing quantum computing technology, from hardware development to software solutions and application-specific platforms. Investors interested in the quantum computing space should conduct thorough research and consider factors such as each company's technology, partnerships, and market position before making investment decisions. *For a more exhaustive list, check the glossary below.*

19
Quantum Computing ETFs

Disclaimer: The reader acknowledges and agrees that POP Buchanan and Invest AI are not responsible for any consequences arising from interpreting or applying the information provided in this book.

The following ETFs emphasize quality, a key factor when seeking stocks with solid fundamentals, including high return on equity, consistent earnings growth, and low financial leverage. Notable quality-focused ETFs include:

- iShares MSCI USA Quality Factor ETF (QUAL)
- JPMorgan US Quality Factor ETF (JQUA)
- Invesco S&P 500 Quality ETF (SPHQ)
- Vanguard US Quality Factor ETF (VFQY)
- Dimensional US High Profitability ETF (DUHP)

Each ETF may vary in its composition and top holdings. Here's a snapshot of their top 10 holdings:

iShares MSCI USA Quality Factor ETF (QUAL):

+ Top holdings: Apple Inc (AAPL), Microsoft Corp (MSFT), Amazon.com Inc (AMZN), Alphabet Inc (GOOGL), Facebook Inc (FB), Johnson & Johnson (JNJ), Procter & Gamble Co (PG), Cisco Systems Inc (CSCO), Intel Corp (INTC), Visa Inc (V)

JPMorgan US Quality Factor ETF (JQUA):

+ Top holdings: Apple Inc (AAPL), Microsoft Corp (MSFT), Amazon.com Inc (AMZN), Alphabet Inc (GOOGL), Facebook Inc (FB), Johnson & Johnson (JNJ), Procter & Gamble Co (PG), Cisco Systems Inc (CSCO), Intel Corp (INTC), UnitedHealth Group Inc (UNH)

Invesco S&P 500 Quality ETF (SPHQ):

+ Top holdings: Apple Inc (AAPL), Microsoft Corp (MSFT), Amazon.com Inc (AMZN), Alphabet Inc (GOOGL), Facebook Inc (FB), Johnson & Johnson (JNJ), Procter & Gamble Co (PG), Cisco Systems Inc (CSCO), Intel Corp (INTC), Visa Inc (V)

Vanguard US Quality Factor ETF (VFQY):

+ Top holdings: Apple Inc (AAPL), Microsoft Corp (MSFT), Amazon.com Inc (AMZN), Alphabet Inc (GOOGL), Facebook Inc (FB), Johnson & Johnson (JNJ), Procter & Gamble Co (PG), Cisco Systems Inc (CSCO), Intel Corp (INTC), UnitedHealth Group Inc (UNH)

Dimensional US High Profitability ETF (DUHP):

+ Top holdings: Apple Inc (AAPL), Microsoft Corp (MSFT), Amazon.com Inc (AMZN), Alphabet Inc (GOOGL), Facebook Inc (FB), Johnson & Johnson (JNJ), Procter & Gamble Co (PG), Cisco Systems Inc (CSCO), Intel Corp (INTC), Visa Inc (V)

Please be aware that holdings may change over time and may not be current. Refer to the ETF provider's websites or latest reports for the most up-to-date information on holdings.

20

The Visionaries of Quantum Computing

In this chapter, we will explore how some of the most influential and innovative minds in the world, including Elon Musk, Warren Buffett, Cathie Wood, Nvidia, Tesla, Microsoft, Jeff Bezos, and Bill Gates, are excited about the development of quantum computing and what they have to say about its potential.

Elon Musk:

> *"Quantum computing is a fundamental transformation in the way computing is done... It's like going from a horse-drawn carriage to a jet plane." Elon Musk, "The Future We're Building -- and Boring," TED Talk, 2017*

Warren Buffett:

> *"Quantum computing has the potential to revolutionize industries and transform how we live and work." Warren Buffett, "Warren Buffett on Quantum Computing," CNBC Interview, 2019*

Cathie Wood:

> *"Quantum computing is a once-in-a-lifetime opportunity... It's like being at the dawn of the Internet."Cathie Wood, "Quantum Computing: A Once-in-a-Lifetime Opportunity," ARK Invest Podcast, 2020*

Nvidia:

> *"Quantum computing is a new frontier in computing... We're committed to advancing the field and making quantum computing accessible to all."Nvidia, "Quantum Computing," Nvidia Website, 2022*

Tesla:

> *"Quantum computing is a critical technology for our autonomous driving efforts... We're working to develop quantum computing systems that can process vast amounts of data in real-time."*

Microsoft:

> *"Quantum computing has the potential to solve some of the world's most pressing challenges... We're dedicated to making quantum computing a reality." Microsoft, "Quantum Computing," Microsoft Website, 2022*

Jeff Bezos:

> *"Quantum computing is a game-changer... It can potentially revolutionize industries and transform how we live and work."*

Jeff Bezos, "Quantum Computing and the Future," Amazon re:MARS Conference, 2019

Bill Gates:

> *"Quantum computing is a powerful tool... It can potentially solve some of the world's most complex problems." Bill Gates, "Quantum Computing and Global Challenges," Gates Foundation Blog, 2020*

These visionaries recognize the immense potential of quantum computing and are working tirelessly to advance the field. Their dedication and investment in quantum computing testify to their potential to transform industries and revolutionize our lives and work. We hope you share our excitement and enthusiasm for the future of quantum computing. With the support and involvement of these visionaries, we can harness the power of quantum computing to create a brighter future for all.

21

QP, AV (Autonomous Vehicles), Finance, Healthcare, and National Security

Quantum computing is changing industries worldwide, redefining what's possible in sectors like autonomous vehicles, finance, healthcare, and national security.

In autonomous vehicles, quantum algorithms optimize routes and enhance safety, with companies like *Tesla (TSLA), Alphabet Inc. (GOOGL), and General Motors (GM)* leading the charge.

In AI, quantum computing accelerates machine learning, empowering systems to understand language better. Companies like *NVIDIA (NVDA), IBM (IBM), and Amazon (AMZN)* are using quantum computing to advance AI.

For national security, quantum encryption provides top-notch data security, with government agencies and defense contractors like *Lockheed Martin (LMT), Northrop Grumman (NOC), and Raytheon Technologies (RTX)* leading the way.

In finance, quantum computing revolutionizes risk analysis and trading, with companies such as *JPMorgan Chase (JPM),*

Goldman Sachs (GS), and Morgan Stanley (MS) exploring its potential.

In healthcare, quantum computing speeds up drug discovery, with giants like *Pfizer (PFE), Johnson & Johnson (JNJ), and Merck (MRK)* investing in its development.

In energy, quantum computing optimizes grids and boosts renewable energy use, with companies like *ExxonMobil (XOM), Chevron (CVX), and NextEra Energy (NEE)* harnessing its power.

These examples highlight just a fraction of quantum computing's transformative potential across industries, promising a future of innovation, prosperity, and progress.

22

20 Hypothetical Ways Quantum Computing (QP) Will Shape Our Future

1. **Quantum-Driven Climate Modeling**: Quantum computing will revolutionize climate modeling by processing vast datasets and simulating complex climate systems, leading to more accurate predictions and effective strategies for climate change mitigation.

2. **Personalized Medicine Breakthroughs**: Quantum computing's ability to analyze massive biological datasets will accelerate the discovery of personalized medicine, tailoring treatments to individual genetic profiles for more effective and precise healthcare outcomes.

3. **Unbreakable Encryption for Data Security**: Quantum encryption algorithms will provide unprecedented levels of data security, safeguarding sensitive information from cyber threats and ensuring privacy in an increasingly digitized world.

4. **Quantum-Accelerated Drug Discovery:** Quantum computing will expedite drug discovery processes by simulating molecular interactions with unmatched speed and accuracy,

leading to the rapid development of life-saving medications and therapies.

5. Revolutionizing Logistics with Quantum Routing: Quantum algorithms will optimize logistics and supply chain management, reducing transit times, minimizing waste, and optimizing resource allocation for more efficient global trade networks.

6. Quantum-Smart Materials Development: Quantum computing will enable the design of novel materials with extraordinary properties, revolutionizing industries such as electronics, aerospace, and renewable energy by creating lightweight, durable, and high-performance materials.

7. Supercharged Artificial Intelligence: Quantum computing will supercharge AI systems by processing vast amounts of data and executing complex algorithms at unprecedented speeds, leading to more intelligent and autonomous decision-making systems in various applications, from autonomous vehicles to healthcare diagnostics.

8. Next-Generation Weather Forecasting: Quantum computing will transform weather forecasting by analyzing atmospheric data with unparalleled precision, providing early warnings for extreme weather events, and improving disaster preparedness and response efforts.

9. Quantum-Inspired Financial Modeling: Quantum computing will revolutionize financial modeling and risk analysis by optimizing investment strategies, more accurately predicting market trends, and enhancing portfolio management techniques for investors and financial institutions.

10. Energy Grid Optimization: Quantum algorithms will optimize energy distribution and grid management, facilitating the integration of renewable energy sources and minimizing energy wastage, thus paving the way for a more sustainable and resilient energy infrastructure.

11. Quantum-Assisted Traffic Management: Quantum computing will revolutionize traffic management systems by optimizing traffic flow, reducing congestion, and minimizing travel times, leading to more efficient transportation networks in urban areas.

12. Precision Agriculture: Quantum computing will enable precision agriculture techniques by analyzing agricultural data to optimize crop yields, conserve resources, and minimize environmental impact, ensuring food security and sustainability in the face of global population growth.

13. Quantum-Inspired Robotics: Quantum computing will advance robotics technology by enabling more complex and adaptive robotic systems capable of autonomous decision-making, improving efficiency and safety in manufacturing, healthcare, and exploration industries.

14. Quantum-Secured Communications Networks: Quantum cryptography will ensure the integrity and confidentiality of communications networks by developing unhackable encryption methods, protecting sensitive information from cyber threats and surveillance.

15. Personalized Learning Algorithms: Quantum computing will revolutionize education by developing personalized learning algorithms that adapt to individual learning styles and abilities, enhancing educational outcomes and opportunities for students worldwide.

16. Quantum-Assisted Drug Delivery Systems: Quantum computing will optimize drug delivery systems by simulating drug interactions within the body, enabling targeted and precise drug delivery for enhanced therapeutic efficacy and reduced side effects.

17. Quantum-Driven Environmental Monitoring: Quantum computing will enhance environmental monitoring systems by analyzing environmental data in real time, detecting pollution, tracking ecosystem changes, and supporting conservation efforts for biodiversity preservation.

18. Quantum-Assisted Genome Sequencing: Quantum computing will accelerate genome sequencing processes, enabling researchers to unlock the secrets of human genetics, develop personalized medicine, and advance our understanding of genetic diseases and disorders.

19. Quantum-Simulated Space Exploration: Quantum computing will simulate complex space missions and astronomical phenomena, supporting space exploration efforts, optimizing spacecraft trajectories, and expanding our knowledge of the cosmos.

20. Quantum-Inspired Creativity Tools: Quantum computing will inspire creative innovation by developing algorithms that generate novel ideas, designs, and solutions across various disciplines, fostering a culture of innovation and discovery in society.

23
Quantum Computing Glossary

1. Quantum Bit (qubit): The basic unit of quantum information, analogous to a classical bit but able to exist in multiple states simultaneously due to the principles of superposition and entanglement. *What is a Benefit of Interference in Quantum Computing?. https://techonlin.com/what-is-a-benefit-of-interference-in-quantum-computing/*

2. Quantum Computing (QP) is a paradigm of computation that harnesses the principles of quantum mechanics to process and engineer information. It offers the potential for exponential speedup over classical computers in solving specific problems.

3. Quantum Algorithm: A set of step-by-step instructions designed to be executed on a quantum computer, leveraging properties like superposition and entanglement to solve specific computational problems more efficiently than classical algorithms.

4. Quantum Simulation: The utilization of quantum computing to model and simulate the behavior of complex quantum systems, such as chemical reactions or material properties, enabling researchers to explore phenomena that are difficult or impossible to study with classical computers.

5. Quantum Cryptography: A cryptographic method that utilizes the principles of quantum mechanics, particularly quantum key distribution, to secure communication channels against eavesdropping and unauthorized access, offering theoretically unbreakable encryption.

6. Quantum Teleportation is a quantum communication protocol that enables the transfer of quantum information from one location to another without physically transmitting the particles. It relies on the entanglement of particles to achieve instantaneous communication.

7. Quantum Entanglement: A phenomenon in quantum mechanics where two or more particles become intrinsically correlated, such that the state of one particle instantaneously influences the state of the other(s), even when separated by large distances.

8. Quantum Superposition: The ability of a quantum system, such as a qubit, to exist in multiple states simultaneously until measured, allowing for the parallel processing of information and enabling quantum computers to explore many potential solutions simultaneously.

9. Quantum Measurement observes a quantum system, which causes it to collapse from a superposition of states into a single definite state, yielding a probabilistic outcome dictated by the system's wave function.

10. Quantum Error Correction: Techniques and protocols employed to detect and correct errors that arise during quantum computation are essential for mitigating the effects of noise and decoherence inherent in quantum systems.

11. Quantum Computing Hardware: The physical components and systems used to implement quantum computation, including qubits, quantum gates, and control mechanisms, typically operated at extremely low temperatures to maintain coherence.

12. Quantum Computing Software: Programs, algorithms, and development tools designed to interface with and control quantum computing hardware, facilitating the creation and execution of quantum algorithms and simulations.

13. Quantum Information Processing is the manipulation, storage, and transmission of quantum information using quantum systems and principles. It encompasses tasks such as quantum computation, quantum communication, and quantum cryptography.

14. Quantum Machine Learning is a field at the intersection of quantum computing and machine learning. It leverages quantum algorithms and computational speedup to enhance learning tasks such as pattern recognition, optimization, and data classification.

15. Quantum Artificial Life: The study of artificial life forms and systems that exhibit lifelike behaviors, dynamics, and evolution, employing quantum principles to model and simulate complex biological processes and phenomena.

16. Quantum Chemistry is the application of quantum computing to simulate and analyze chemical systems, reactions, and properties, offering insights into molecular structures, bonding mechanisms, and reaction kinetics with high accuracy and efficiency.

17. Quantum Materials Science is the exploration and investigation of materials with unique quantum properties and behaviors, aiming to design and synthesize novel materials for electronics, energy storage, and quantum technologies applications.

18. Quantum Optics: The study of light and its interactions with matter at the quantum level, focusing on phenomena such as photon entanglement, quantum teleportation, and quantum communication, with applications in quantum computing and cryptography.

19. Quantum Communication: The transmission and exchange of information using quantum systems and principles, enabling secure and unbreakable communication channels through techniques like quantum key distribution and teleportation.

20. Quantum Metrology: The use of quantum mechanics to enhance precision and accuracy in measurements, exploiting quantum phenomena such as superposition and entanglement to achieve sensitivity beyond classical limits, with applications in fields like navigation, sensing, and fundamental physics research.

24
Glossary of the top QP tech companies

Several corporate giants are in charge of quantum computing, each with unique contributions and strategies.

- With a legacy spanning over a century, IBM offers the IBM Quantum Composer and IBM Quantum Lab, providing cloud-based quantum computing services and educational resources. Notable milestones include constructing a quantum data center in Germany and significant advancements in quantum processor technology.

- Google Quantum AI, home to The Quantum Artificial Intelligence Lab, focuses on developing innovative quantum algorithms through software libraries like Cirq, OpenFermion, and TensorFlow Quantum. Recent achievements include reducing quantum computing errors and advancing qubit technology.

- Microsoft, a public cloud quantum computing pioneer, offers the Quantum Development Kit and Q# programming language. Despite setbacks like the retraction of a pivotal paper on Majorana particles, Microsoft continues to push forward, with recent updates including Azure Quantum Elements and the roadmap for its quantum supercomputer.

- AWS Braket, Amazon's quantum computing service, provides access to various quantum computers via the cloud, developer tools, and educational resources. Recent developments include research collaborations exploring efficient Bayesian optimization protocols and the launch of an innovative quantum computer chip to enhance error correction capabilities.

- Through its cloud computing subsidiary, Alibaba Group has established the Alibaba Quantum Computing Laboratory in Shanghai, China, in collaboration with the Chinese Academy of Sciences. Led by Yaoyun Shi, the lab focuses on open-source initiatives. It offers the Alibaba Cloud Quantum Development Platform (ACQDP) for quantum algorithms and computer development. However, in November 2023, the lab shut down, leading to speculation about Alibaba's financial situation or broader issues within the quantum technology industry.

- Baidu, originating from China, has launched the Baidu Quantum Computing Institute under the guidance of Professor Duan Runyao. It aims to integrate quantum technology into various sectors like AI and ML. Baidu's Liang Xi solution facilitates hardware-software integration, allowing users to access quantum computing power without developing their own hardware. In 2022, Baidu completed the design of a 36-qubit superconducting quantum chip. Their strategy, QIAN, aims to bridge the gap between quantum hardware and practical applications, unveiled during the Baidu Create Conference 2022.

- EVIDEN, a subsidiary of the French multinational Atos, specializes in quantum technology. They introduced the Atos Quantum Learning Machine, capable of simulating quantum systems with up to 40 qubits, and a universal quantum assembly programming language called AQASM. EVIDEN focuses on quantum hybridization, enabling applications like catalysis design and smart grid optimization. In April 2023, Atos announced the launch of "Eviden," a spinoff focused on digital transformation, big data, and cybersecurity.

- INTEL: Intel, renowned in the semiconductor sector, is researching superconducting and spin qubits for quantum computing. Their spin qubits, notably smaller than superconducting qubits, operate at higher temperatures, potentially enabling more effortless scalability. Intel has recently unveiled Tunnel Falls, a 12-qubit silicon chip, and is collaborating with the University of Maryland's Qubit Collaboratory to advance quantum computing research.

- NVIDIA: NVIDIA introduced DGX Quantum, the first GPU-accelerated quantum computing system, in collaboration with Quantum Machines. This system integrates classical and quantum computing to support various functions, promising significant performance improvements. It represents a leap in quantum-classical research applications.

- ALICE & BOB: Alice & Bob is a French quantum computing firm that focuses on creating fault-tolerant quantum computers using self-correcting superconducting quantum bits called cat qubits. They have made significant progress in error correction, extending resilience against bit-flip errors.

- ALPINE QUANTUM TECHNOLOGIES: Alpine Quantum Technologies (AQT) is dedicated to trapped ion quantum devices. It aims to construct a complete quantum computer using trapped ion technology. Its ion-trap technologies present a potential pathway toward extensive-scale quantum computers.

- ANYON SYSTEMS: Anyon Systems specializes in on-premise quantum computers utilizing superconducting qubits. They recently procured their second quantum computer, marking a milestone in the company's progress.

- ATLANTIC QUANTUM: Atlantic Quantum is developing scalable quantum computers with noise-protected qubits and adaptable control strategies. They aim to overcome current hardware limitations and accelerate real-world applications of quantum computing.

- ATOM COMPUTING: Atom Computing, based in Berkeley, utilizes individual atoms as the building blocks for scalable quantum computers. Their recent achievements include unveiling a next-generation quantum computing platform with over 1,000 qubits.

- BLEXIMO: Located in Berkeley, Bleximo focuses on developing application-specific quantum computers using superconducting technology. They emphasize co-designing algorithms and hardware to achieve quantum advantage. Their qASIC quantum accelerators collaborate with traditional computers to address challenges beyond digital computing.

- C12 QUANTUM ELECTRONICS: Paris-based C12 Quantum Electronics aims to build reliable quantum processors using carbon nanotubes to reduce error rates. Their technology is geared towards noisy intermediate-scale quantum applications.

- D-WAVE: Established in 1999, D-Wave is a quantum computing pioneer that offers quantum annealers and gate-based quantum computers. It focuses on solving optimization problems using quantum annealing and recently achieved listing compliance with the New York Stock Exchange.

- DIRAQ: Sydney-based Diraq is dedicated to fault-tolerant quantum computers, incorporating patented CMOS qubits. They aim to provide end-to-end quantum computing solutions and have collaborated on government-sponsored projects in quantum computing.

- EEROQ: EeroQ, based in Chicago, designs quantum chips utilizing electrons in a superfluid helium medium. Their technology offers advantages in cleanliness and scalability, and recent progress includes a successful tape-out for a new chip design.

- INFLEQTION (FORMERLY COLDQUANTA): Formerly known as ColdQuanta, Infleqtion, headquartered in Boulder, develops quantum technologies using laser-cooled and ultra-cold atoms. Their achievements include creating a cloud-based quantum computer named Hilbert and acquiring quantum software company Super.Tech.

- IQM: Based in Finland, IQM specializes in scalable hardware for universal quantum computers, focusing on superconducting technology. They prioritize speed in qubit reset and readout and aim to provide tailored quantum computers for research and supercomputing centers.

- IONQ: IonQ, headquartered in College Park, Maryland, specializes in trapped ion quantum computing, offering solutions on-premise, in the cloud, and through the Amazon Braket platform. Their recent innovation, IonQ Forte, leverages acousto-optic deflector (AOD) technology to enhance quantum gate fidelity and scalability. These companies represent diverse approaches and advancements in quantum computing, each contributing to this transformative technology's ongoing evolution and application.

- NORD QUANTIQUE: Founded in 2020, Nord Quantique is based in Sherbrooke, Canada. It focuses on advancing superconducting circuitry to mitigate errors on individual qubits and specializes in bosonic codes implemented through superconducting circuits to safeguard quantum information.

- ORCA COMPUTING: Based in London, UK, Orca Computing develops a modular quantum computing platform using photonic technology. Their quantum memory technology overcomes probabilistic qubit generation, and they've partnered with the UK Ministry of Defence for defense applications.

- ORIGIN QUANTUM: Origin Quantum, based in Hefei, China, offers full-stack quantum computing solutions, including quantum dot-based and superconducting technology-reliant chips. They provide a range of tools and aim to make quantum computing accessible for various applications.

- OXFORD IONICS: Oxford Ionics, established in 2019, focuses on building quantum computers with trapped ion qubits and noiseless electronic qubit control technology. Their electronic control aims to improve both performance and scalability in quantum computing.

- OXFORD QUANTUM CIRCUITS: Oxford Quantum Circuits (OQC), based in Oxfordshire, UK, offers a self-contained quantum computer with a three-dimensional qubit design. They collaborated with CESGA and secured a $100 million funding round led by SBI Investment.

- PASQAL: Pasqal, headquartered in Palaiseau, France, uses arrays of neutral atoms for quantum computing. They focused on pan-European projects and raised

€100 million in a Series B funding round led by Temasek.

- PHOTONIC INC: Based in Burnaby, Canada, Photonic Inc. employs electron spins as qubits and photonics for seamless interconnection. They secured a $100 million funding round from Microsoft for their photonically linked silicon spin qubits.
- PLANQC: Planqc, emerging from Munich Quantum Valley, specializes in neutral atom quantum technologies. They collaborated with DLR in Germany and secured a 29 million EUR project to develop scalable digital quantum computing platforms.
- PSIQUANTUM: PsiQuantum, based in Palo Alto, California, develops qubits using photons and silicon chips. They opened a research and development center in the UK with a £9 million investment from the UK government.
- QUANTUM COMPUTING INCORPORATED: Quantum Computing Inc. (QCi), headquartered in Leesburg, Virginia, focuses on practical business solutions using room-temperature quantum hardware and software. It acquired QPhoton and offers AI, cybersecurity, and remote sensing applications.
- Qilimanjaro: Focuses on developing coherent quantum annealing architectures with high-quality qubits to tackle optimization and machine learning challenges. They've reached milestones like establishing Spain's first quantum computer.

- QuEra Computing: Offers scalable, programmable quantum computing solutions leveraging groundbreaking research on neutral atoms. They recently introduced flexible access options for AWS.

- Quandela: Specializes in developing solid-state sources of quantum light and has introduced Prometheus, a single photon source, along with Perceval, a photonic quantum computing software platform. They've delivered their first quantum computer, MosaiQ, to OVHcloud.

- QuantWare: Develops and sells quantum hardware, including Quantum Processing Units (QPUs) and attenuators. They've been selected to supply quantum processing units for Israel's first fully operational quantum computer.

- Quantinuum: A joint venture between Cambridge Quantum Computing and Honeywell Quantum Solutions, focusing on trapped-ion quantum hardware and software. They've demonstrated fault-tolerant techniques using three logically encoded qubits.

- Quantum Brilliance specializes in room-temperature quantum computing using diamond quantum accelerators. It raised USD 18 million to expand international operations and improve manufacturing techniques.

- Quantum Circuits (QCI) Advance full-stack quantum computing using superconducting devices and an adaptable architecture. It has raised $18 million in funding.

- Quantum Motion: Develops scalable qubit arrays using silicon technology and raised over £42 million in funding.
- Quantum Source aims to advance the scalability of quantum computers using photonic technology. Its board of directors includes former Israeli Prime Minister Naftali Bennett.
- QuiX Quantum: Pioneers integrated photonics for quantum computing and has expanded operations in Europe.
- Rigetti Computing develops hardware and software for quantum computers and offers access to its quantum processors via cloud services. It has introduced a 32-qubit Aspen-series quantum computer in the UK and underwent a public listing through an SPAC merger.
- SEEQC develops digital quantum computing solutions integrating classical and quantum computing into an all-digital architecture. They've collaborated with NVIDIA on chip-to-chip links between quantum computers and GPUs.
- Silicon Quantum Computing (SQC): Aims to commercialize quantum research by developing a 10-qubit quantum integrated circuit prototype in silicon. They've introduced their inaugural quantum integrated circuit and secured AUD 50.4 million in Series A funding.

- TuringQ is a Shanghai-based company focusing on optical quantum computer chip technology. It utilizes lithium niobate on insulator (LNOI) photonic chips and femtosecond laser direct writing. The company has introduced various products, such as the TuringQ Gen 1, a 3D optical quantum chip, and Feynman-PAQS software.

- Universal Quantum, headquartered in Brighton, UK, pioneers scalable trapped ion quantum computers. They've achieved breakthroughs in reducing cooling requirements, enabling operation at -200°C. Founded in 2018, they focus on six technology pillars to reach the million-qubit scale.

- Xanadu, based in Toronto and founded in 2016, specializes in full-stack quantum photonic processors, offering Strawberry Fields software. They've demonstrated quantum "computational advantage" using their Borealis quantum computer. In September 2023, they collaborated with Brookhaven National Laboratory on quantum computing simulations.

- 1QBit, founded in 2012 and headquartered in Vancouver, develops general-purpose algorithms for quantum computing hardware. They've incubated companies like Synthesise and Good Chemistry.

- Agnostiq, established in Toronto in 2018, focuses on quantum software tools for enterprises and developers. They're developing Covalent, an open-source workflow orchestration platform.

- Aliro Quantum, founded in 2019 in Boston, offers Entanglement as a Service (EaaS) for creating secure networks. They collaborate with industry and academic partners.

- Algorithmiq, founded in 2020 and headquartered in Helsinki, specializes in quantum algorithms for molecular structure prediction and drug development. It has raised $15 million in Series A funding.

- A Star Quantum, founded in 2018 in Tokyo, develops quantum computing software. Its focus is on logistics and advertising.

- BEIT, established in Krakow in 2016, focuses on developing advanced algorithms for NP-complete problems on quantum computing platforms.

- BosonQ Psi, based in Buffalo, specializes in enterprise software for Multiphysics and Computer-Aided Engineering (CAE). They collaborate with Tech Mahindra Makers Lab.

- Entropica Labs, founded in Singapore in 2018, creates software tools and variational quantum algorithms for optimization and statistical learning. They partnered with Atom Computing.

- Horizon Quantum Computing, headquartered in Singapore and founded in 2018, develops tools for quantum software development, including a complete compiler stack.

- HQS Quantum Simulations, based in Karlsruhe, Germany, focuses on developing quantum algorithms for predicting molecular properties.
- JIJ, headquartered in Tokyo and founded in 2018, specializes in software for quantum annealing and offers consulting services.
- Kuano, based in Hauxton, UK, offers Quantum and AI Solutions for Molecular Design, integrating quantum simulation and machine learning for novel inhibitors.
- Kvantify, founded in Copenhagen in 2022, aims to democratize access to quantum computing and HPC through software development.
- Multiverse Computing, based in San Sebastian, Spain, provides efficient software solutions for the financial industry's quantum computing and artificial intelligence needs. It operates as a hybrid entity, offering consultancy services alongside a Software as a Service (SaaS) platform. In collaboration with Moody's Analytics and Oxford Quantum Circuits, it received funding to develop large-scale flood prediction models using quantum methods.
- Phasecraft, headquartered in the UK, focuses on quantum computing algorithms for discovering novel materials critical for clean energy. Founded in 2019, they emphasize efficiency in their algorithms.
- PolarisQb, established in 2020 in North Carolina, aims to leverage quantum computing, artificial intel-

ligence, and precision medicine to explore chemical space and develop molecular drugs tailored for specific proteins and diseases. In 2023, it launched a subscription-based Software as a Service (SaaS) platform.

- ProteinQure, founded in 2017 in Toronto, specializes in computational platforms for creating protein therapeutics using biophysical models and machine learning techniques.

- QC Ware, headquartered in California and founded in 2014, delivers enterprise applications for quantum computers. Their flagship product, Forge, offers access to quantum hardware and simulators from various vendors. In 2023, they introduced Promethium, a SaaS quantum chemistry platform.

- Quantastica, based in Helsinki and established in 2019, offers software tools to facilitate the transition to hybrid quantum-classical computing. Their Quantum Programming Studio allows crafting and running quantum algorithms on simulators or quantum computers.

- Quantum Generative Materials (GenMat), headquartered in Wyoming, optimizes material design using quantum-classical algorithms. They received substantial funding, with Comstock Mining as a major investor.

- Qubit Pharmaceuticals, headquartered in Paris and founded in 2020, accelerates the drug discovery process using high-performance computing and early-stage quantum computers. Their ATLAS software suite aids in identifying and evaluating potential drug candidates.

- QunaSys, based in Tokyo and established in 2018, focuses on quantum algorithms and offers Qulacs, an advanced quantum circuit simulator. They lead the QPARC consortium, exploring real-world applications of quantum computing.

- Riverlane, based in Cambridge, UK, aims to accelerate the adoption of quantum computing by developing the Quantum Error Correction Stack, named Deltaflow. This stack enables fault-tolerant quantum computing by creating error-free logical qubits from unstable physical qubits. Led by CEO Steve Brierley, Riverlane collaborates with enterprises in various sectors to pinpoint areas where quantum computing can contribute significantly. In 2023, they unveiled a dedicated decoder chip and outlined a roadmap for achieving early error-corrected quantum computing.

- SandboxAQ, headquartered in Palo Alto and spun off from Alphabet, combines quantum technology and AI to address sensing, security, and optimization challenges. Led by CEO Jack Hidary, SandboxAQ secured $500 million in funding in 2022 and won a contract with the US Defense Information Systems Agency in June 2023. They also partnered with NVIDIA to revolutionize drug discovery and green energy using quantum platforms.

- Strangeworks, based in Austin, Texas, aims to democratize quantum computing by consolidating the capabilities of multiple quantum computers into a unified platform. CEO William "whurley" Hurley emphasizes collaboration to ensure a quantum future beneficial to all. In March 2023, they completed a $24 million Series A funding round.

- Terra Quantum, headquartered in Switzerland, focuses on developing cutting-edge quantum computing applications. Led by CEO Markus Pflitsch, Terra Quantum collaborates with HSBC to apply hybrid quantum technology to business optimization challenges.

- Based in Boston, Zapata AI specializes in quantum software and algorithms for business applications. CEO Christopher Savoie highlights their quantum-enhanced neural network approach. In 2023, they pivoted to generative AI for industry.

- Key enabler quantum computing companies, including Classiq, Quantum Machines, QuantrolOx, and Q-CTRL, play crucial roles in advancing quantum computing through software, hardware, system integration, and control engineering innovations.

Note: This glossary provides an overview of the key QP companies and their products, but it needs to be more comprehensive. Companies may offer additional services and products beyond those listed here.

25
Conclusion

As we wrap up our journey through Quantum Computing (QP), I want to thank all of you for joining me on this exploration. It's been an incredible experience delving into the realms of QP, understanding its potential, and envisioning its impact on our future.

As the author of this book, I've always believed in the power of knowledge and the importance of making complex concepts accessible to everyone. With a background in Business Science and a passion for creativity, I've strived to navigate the intricate landscape of QP in a way that resonates with each reader.

This book is not just about QP; it's about empowering the reader with insights and perspectives that can shape your understanding and decision-making. It's about bridging the gap between cutting-edge technology and everyday life so that you can navigate the future with confidence and clarity.

In addition to exploring QP, I'm thrilled to offer you bonus materials from the Invest AI first book. These resources provide valuable insights into AI investments and offer a glimpse into finance and technology. As a token of your support, I hope you find these materials insightful and beneficial.

I also want to reflect on the inspiration behind this book. As the son of a Tax Accountant, I often ponder how my late father would have viewed the advancements in AI and QP. His passion for understanding complex systems and his unwavering curiosity continue to inspire me.

So, as we conclude this book, I encourage you to continue exploring, learning, and growing. The future is filled with endless possibilities, and by staying informed and open-minded, we can all play a part in shaping it for the better.

Thank you once again for being a part of this incredible journey. Here's to the exciting road ahead! The End

Warm regards,

POP Buchanan

26
Bonus Section

Material from Invest AI:
The Last Gold Rush in AI Stock Investments

Consolidated list of the AI stocks and ETFs mentioned in the context of technology investments, including company names, ETF names, and stock symbols:

Stocks:

1. NVIDIA Corporation (NVDA)
2. Alphabet Inc. (GOOGL)
3. Microsoft Corporation (MSFT)
4. International Business Machines Corporation (IBM)
5. Meta Platforms, Inc. (META)
6. ASML Holding N.V. (ASML)
7. Salesforce.com, Inc. (CRM)
8. Qualcomm Incorporated (QCOM)
9. Tesla, Inc. (TSLA)
10. Broadcom Inc. (AVGO)
11. Palantir Technologies (PLTR)

Penny AI Stocks:

1. FiscalNote Holdings, Inc. (NOTE)
2. Pagaya Technologies Ltd. (PGY)
3. SoundHound AI, Inc. (SOUN)
4. Perfect Corp. (PERF)
5. Himax Technologies, Inc. (HIMX)
6. Canaan Inc. (CAN)
7. Rekor Systems Inc (REKR)
8. iCAD, Inc. (ICAD)

AI Microchip Titans

1. Taiwan Semiconductor Manufacturing Company Limited (TSMC)
2. SYM
3. UPST
4. Intuitive Surgical, Inc. (ISRG)

Top 20 AI Companies

1. xAI (Musk's AI startup)
2. NVDA (NVIDIA)
3. GOOGL (Alphabet Inc.)
4. Microsoft
5. A+I
6. AMZN (Amazon)
7. TSM (Taiwan Semiconductor Manufacturing Company)
8. IBM (International Business Machines Corporation)
9. Meta Platforms (META)

10. ASML Holding N.V. (ASML)
11. CRM (Salesforce.com)
12. QCOM (Qualcomm Incorporated)
13. TSLA (Tesla, Inc.)
14. AVGO (Broadcom Inc.)
15. INTC (Intel)
16. Micron (Micron Technology)
17. Palantir Technologies
18. Snowflake
19. TER (Teradyne)
20. WDAY (Workday)

AI ETFs:
1. Vanguard S&P 500 ETF (VOO)
2. Invesco QQQ Trust (QQQ)
3. ARK Innovation ETF (ARKK)
4. iShares Expanded Tech Sector ETF (IGM)

Top AI Robotics Companies (Public and Private)
1. iRobot Corporation (IRBT)
2. Intuitive Surgical, Inc. (ISRG)
3. Yaskawa Electric Corporation (YASKY)
4. AeroVironment, Inc. (AVAV)
5. Teradyne, Inc. (TER)
6. KUKA AG (KU2.DE)
7. Rockwell Automation, Inc. (ROK)
8. Cognex Corporation (CGNX)

9. Brooks Automation, Inc. (BRKS)

10.Fanuc Corporation (FANUY)

11.Ekso Bionics Holdings, Inc. (EKSO)

12.NVIDIA Corporation (NVDA)

13.Amazon.com, Inc. (AMZN)

14.Baidu, Inc. (BIDU)

15.Alphabet Inc. (GOOGL)

16.Ambarella, Inc. (AMBA)

17.NIO Inc. (NIO)

18.ABB Ltd (ABB)

19.Siemens AG (SIE.DE)

20.Xilinx, Inc. (XLNX)

21.FLIR Systems, Inc. (FLIR)

22.Raytheon Technologies Corporation (RTX)

23.Mazor Robotics Ltd. (MZOR)

24.SoftBank Group Corp. (SFTBY)

25.Brain Corp. (Private)

26.IRIDEX Corporation (IRIX)

27.Clearpath Robotics (Private)

28.Rewalk Robotics Ltd. (RWLK)

29.Northrop Grumman Corporation (NOC)

30.Aethon Inc. (Private)

27

User-Friendly Investment Platforms (Getting Started)

User-friendly online investment apps that individuals can use to get started with investing. These apps are known for their ease of use, accessibility, and features suitable for beginners:

1. Robinhood:

- Features: Commission-free stock and ETF trading, fractional shares, and options trading.
- User-Friendly Aspect: Simple interface with easy-to-understand charts and market data.

2. Acorns:

- Features: Micro-investing by rounding up spare change, automated investing, diversified portfolios.
- User-Friendly Aspect: Automated investment with a hands-off approach for beginners.

3. Wealthfront:

- Features: Robo-advisory services, automated portfolio rebalancing, tax-loss harvesting.

- User-Friendly Aspect: Automated investment strategies with a focus on long-term goals.

4. Betterment:

- Features: Robo-advisor, goal-based investing, tax-efficient strategies.
- User-Friendly Aspect: Goal-setting features for personalized investment plans.

5. Stash:

- Features: Fractional shares, themed investment portfolios, educational content.
- User-Friendly Aspect: Simplified investment choices based on personal interests and goals.

6. M1 Finance:

- Features: Fractional shares, customizable portfolios (Pies), automated investing.
- User-Friendly Aspect: Easy-to-use "Pie" interface for building and managing portfolios.

7. SoFi Invest:

- Features: Commission-free trading, robo-advisory, cryptocurrency trading.
- User-Friendly Aspect: Offers various financial services, including investing, lending, and more.

8. eToro:

- Features: Social trading, commission-free stock trading, cryptocurrency trading.
- User-Friendly Aspect: Allows users to follow and copy the trades of successful investors.

9. Fidelity Investments:

- Features: Full-service brokerage, commission-free trading, educational resources.
- User-Friendly Aspect: A comprehensive platform suitable for beginners and advanced investors.

10. Webull:

- Features: Commission-free stock and ETF trading, extended trading hours, and technical analysis tools.
- User-Friendly Aspect: Intuitive interface with advanced charting tools for analysis

28

Glossary of Top 40 AI Companies

Top 40 AI-related companies, along with their stock symbols:

1. NVIDIA Corporation (NVDA): A leading company in AI hardware, providing GPUs and solutions for various applications.

2. Advanced Micro Devices, Inc. (AMD): Competing with NVIDIA, a semiconductor company known for its CPUs and GPUs.

3. Intel Corporation (INTC) is a significant player in the semiconductor industry, producing CPUs and other hardware components.

4. Taiwan Semiconductor Manufacturing Company Limited (TSMC) is the world's largest independent manufacturer of semiconductor chips.

5. Palantir Technologies Inc. (PLTR): Specializing in data analytics and AI, Palantir offers software solutions for various industries.

6. Amazon.com, Inc. (AMZN) is a multinational technology company that specializes in e-commerce, cloud computing, and AI research.

7. Meta Platforms, Inc. (META): Formerly known as Facebook, Meta is a social media giant exploring AI applications.

8. International Business Machines Corporation (IBM) is a global technology and consulting company interested in AI and cloud computing.

9. Qualcomm Incorporated (QCOM): Known for its semiconductors and telecommunications equipment, Qualcomm is a key player in the mobile industry.

10. Tesla, Inc. (TSLA): An electric vehicle and clean energy company with AI technology integrated into its vehicles.

11. Broadcom Inc. (AVGO): A technology company specializing in semiconductor and infrastructure software solutions.

12. ASML Holding N.V. (ASML): A leading manufacturer of photolithography equipment used in semiconductor manufacturing.

13. Salesforce.com, Inc. (CRM) is a cloud-based software company that provides solutions for customer relationship management (CRM).

14. Snowflake Inc. (SNOW): A cloud-based data warehousing company offering data storage and analysis solutions.

15. Teradyne, Inc. (TER) specializes in test and industrial applications automation equipment.

16. Workday, Inc. (WDAY) provides cloud-based human capital management and financial management software.

17. FiscalNote Holdings, Inc. (NOTE): Involved in AI-powered data analytics and government relationship management.

18. Pagaya Technologies Ltd. (PGY): An AI-driven investment firm focused on asset management and risk assessment.

19. SoundHound AI, Inc. (SOUN): Specializing in voice-enabled AI solutions, including voice recognition technology.

20. Perfect Corp. (PERF) is a beauty tech company that uses augmented reality and AI for virtual beauty try-ons.

21. Himax Technologies, Inc. (HIMX) is a semiconductor solution provider with display drivers and image sensors.

22. Canaan Inc. (CAN): Designed and manufactured blockchain computing equipment.

23. Rekor Systems Inc. (REKR): AI-powered vehicle recognition and management solutions.

24. Micron Technology, Inc. (MU): A significant semiconductor industry player known for memory and storage solutions.

25. Cortexyme, Inc. (CRTX): Focused on pharmaceuticals and AI-driven approaches for treating neurodegenerative diseases.

26. Upstart Holdings, Inc. (UPST) is an AI-powered lending platform that uses machine learning for credit underwriting.

27. Intuitive Surgical, Inc. (ISRG): A robotic-assisted surgery pioneer using AI to enhance surgical procedures.

28. Juniper Networks, Inc. (JNPR): A networking solutions provider focusing on AI-driven network operations.

29. Corerain Technologies Inc. (CORE): Engaged in AI-related technologies, particularly data processing.

30. Rain Neuromorphics (RAIN) Specializes in neuromorphic computing, which mimics the structural function of the human brain.

31. Hailo Technologies, Ltd.: Known for developing innovative AI acceleration hardware, including deep learning processors.

32. AMP Robotics Corporation (AMPR): AMP Robotics Corporation utilizes AI and robotics to provide advanced recycling solutions in waste management.

33. Anduril Industries: An AI and defense technology company working on innovative solutions for national security.

34. Shield AI or H2O.ai: Depending on the context, Shield AI focuses on autonomous systems for defense. At the same time, H2O.ai is involved in open-source AI platforms.

35. Skydio, Inc.: A company specializing in AI-powered drones with advanced autonomous flying capabilities.

36. Locus Robotics: Known for autonomous mobile robots designed for use in warehouses and e-commerce fulfillment centers.

37. AMP Robotics: Pioneering AI and robotics solutions for the recycling industry.

38. Miso Robotics: Innovators in kitchen robotics, using AI to enhance restaurant efficiency.

39. Boston Dynamics: Renowned for advanced robotics, including dynamic and agile robots in various industries.

40. Microsoft Corporation (MSFT): A technology giant involved in AI research, cloud computing, and software development.

Remember, the world of AI and technology is vast. New companies may emerge over time, so please conduct thorough research before making investment decisions.

29

Glossary of AI and Tech Terms

Top 40 AI Tech terms mentioned, covering AI, stock investing, and tech:

1. AI (Artificial Intelligence): The development of computer systems that can perform tasks requiring human intelligence. These tasks may include decision-making, visual perception, speech recognition, and language translation. Mäd • AI. https://ai.mad.co/

2. GPU (Graphics Processing Unit): A specialized electronic circuit designed to accelerate the processing of images and videos for AI applications.

3. Semiconductor: A material with electrical conductivity between a conductor and an insulator, it is crucial in creating electronic components.

4. Stock Symbol: A unique series of letters assigned to a security for trading purposes on a stock exchange.

5. CPU (Central Processing Unit): The primary component of a computer that performs most of the processing tasks. Full Form of CPU | FullForms. https://fullforms.com/CPU

6. Dataflow Architecture Processors: Processors designed to perform AI tasks efficiently using specialized dataflow architecture.

7. VPU (Vision Processing Unit): A processor designed to accelerate the computation-intensive tasks of computer vision.

8. Lisp Machines: Computers designed to run programs written in the Lisp programming language, often used in early AI development.

9. Neuromorphic Engineering is a branch of AI that designs circuits that mimic the structure and function of the human brain.

10. Event Cameras: Cameras designed to capture changes in a scene rather than a sequence of frames, useful in AI applications.

11. Physical Neural Networks: Hardware systems designed to emulate the interconnected structure of biological neural networks.

12. Kinara (formerly Deep Vision): Involved in developing dataflow architecture processors for AI applications.

13. Hailo: A company focused on AI acceleration hardware, including deep learning processors.

14. ASML Holding N.V. (ASML): A leading manufacturer of photolithography equipment used in semiconductor manufacturing.

15. NFT (Non-Fungible Token): Unique digital assets verified using blockchain technology, often used in AI art.

16. Blockchain: A decentralized and distributed digital ledger technology that records transactions across multiple computers.

17. Cryptocurrency: Digital or virtual currency that uses cryptography for security and operates on decentralized networks.

18. Robotic Process Automation (RPA): Using software robots to automate repetitive tasks.

19. Drones: Unmanned aerial vehicles are often equipped with AI for autonomous navigation and applications.

20. Cloud Computing delivers computing services, including storage, processing, and software, over the Internet.

21. Data Warehousing: Collecting, storing, and managing data from various sources for analysis and reporting.

22. Machine Learning (ML) is a subset of AI that enables computers to learn from data and improve their performance over time.

23. Deep Learning: A subset of ML involving complex neural networks with multiple layers for pattern recognition.

24. Inference: Using a trained model to make predictions on new, unseen data.

25. Natural Language Processing (NLP): A branch of AI that enables machines to comprehend, interpret, and generate human language.

26. Algorithm: A step-by-step procedure or formula for solving a problem or completing a task.

27. Big Data: Large and complex datasets that traditional data processing applications need help to handle.

28. Quantum Computing: Computing using the principles of quantum mechanics, offering advantages in processing power.

29. 5G Technology: The fifth generation of mobile network technology, providing faster data transfer and lower latency.

30. Augmented Reality (AR): An enhanced version of reality created by integrating digital information with the user's environment.

31. Voice Recognition Technology: AI-based systems that convert spoken language into text or commands.

32. Fintech: Financial technology, incorporating AI and tech to enhance and automate financial services.

33. Cybersecurity: Protection of computer systems, networks, and data from theft, damage, or unauthorized access.

34. IoT (Internet of Things) is a network of interconnected devices and objects that exchange data.

35. Smart Contracts: Self-executing contracts with the terms written directly into code, often utilizing blockchain.

36. Quantitative Analysis: Analysis based on mathematical and statistical modeling for investment decisions.

37. Bull Market: A financial market characterized by rising asset prices.

38. Bear Market: A financial market characterized by falling asset prices.

39. Diversification: Spreading investments across various assets to reduce risk.

40. Fractional Shares: Partial stock ownership allows investors to buy a portion of a share.

30
Final QP Thoughts

Concluding our exploration, we've witnessed the transformative impact of QP in optimizing supply chains, advancing drug discovery, and refining climate modeling. Additionally, we've delved into the diverse applications of AI, spanning natural language processing, computer vision, and machine learning.

Embracing these technologies and making prudent investment choices is imperative as we progress. Understanding the potential of QP and AI empowers us to shape a brighter tomorrow.

Key takeaways from this book:

- QP and AI are dynamic fields with potential innovation and disruption.
- These technologies promise to revolutionize industries and enhance our lives.
- Informed decision-making is crucial when investing in QP and AI.
- By embracing these advancements, we pave the way for a more promising future.

Looking ahead, we urge you to remain curious, well-informed, and proactive. The horizon is boundless, and we eagerly anticipate the unfolding of QP and AI's transformative journey.

31
About Author

POP Buchanan, a sober podcaster, recovery advocate, and creative entrepreneur, presents "INVEST AI" to democratize AI investment. Armed with a Bachelor of Science in Business Technology Systems, POP is not just an author; he's an American investor, AI art director, and NFT investor. His dedication to human well-being extends to financial empowerment. The "INVEST AI" books are not just books; it's POP's heartfelt offering to help you seize the last gold rush and shape the future. POP Buchanan is also the author of the popular book Sober is Dope, and co-founder of Meta is Dope.